AGING WEL'

M000117702

THE NEW R & R:
RETIRED AND REWIRED

PETER MENCONI

MT. SAGE PUBLISHING

Mt. Sage Publishing
Centennial, CO 80122

Copyright © 2013 by Peter Menconi. All rights reserved. No part of this book may be reproduced in any form without written permission from Peter Menconi.

Scriptures taken from the Holy Bible, New International Version®, NIV®. Copyright © 1973, 1978, 1984, 2011 by Biblica, Inc.™ Used by permission of Zondervan. All rights reserved worldwide. www.zondervan.com The "NIV" and "New International Version" are trademarks registered in the United States Patent and Trademark Office by Biblica, Inc.™

TABLE OF CONTENTS

ABOUT THE CASA NETWORK

In 1983, three Southern California churches established the CASA Network ministry to serve their 50+ members through cooperative efforts. The first jointly sponsored one day event was called Jamboree (now Life Celebration). The response to this first event led to a three day retreat held at a Christian conference center. A committee representing various churches met the next year to discover how to meet the growing needs of the Christian adult senior community and to discuss incorporating. They determined that the name of the new organization would be called CASA, Christian Association of Senior Adults.

In 1993 the CASA Board of Directors caught the vision to broaden its ministry to mid and post career age men and women nationally and internationally. In the fall of 1994, CASA launched two quarterly publications – The Energizer for senior adults and Energizing Leaders for leaders of Adults 50+ in the local church. With the explosion of the Boomer generation, a third quarterly publication was launched in 2001 for this population, called Legacy Living. For a time, CASA engaged in a website partnership with Christianity Today.

From 1993 through 1998 regional leadership training conferences were offered to pastors and lay leaders of adult 50+ ministries in a number of states and Canada. In 1998, the first National Leadership Training Conference was held in Irvine, CA and brought together over 300 pastors and lay leaders from 26 states and Canada. A further development in the growth of CASA's ministry was the establishment of a website **www.gocasa.org** that provides resources and information on 50+ ministry. Serving leaders across the country, the CASA Network offers regional, national, and international 50+ leadership conferences. You can access the CASA Network website at **www.gocasa.org** for the latest information on training offerings.

Today, the CASA Network is a premier training and equipping source for the Church's ministry to midlife and beyond age men and women. Augmented by internet and print media, the CASA Network brings together an array of leaders within the field of 50+ ministry to inspire and equip the Church for ministry to and through adults in life's second half. Only God knows how many lives have been touched, how many churches have been changed, how many leaders have been trained because of the vision and leadership of the CASA Network. Check us out at **www.gocasa.org** and welcome to the CASA Network Aging Well Bible Study Series.

BEFORE YOU BEGIN!
Instructions on how to get the most out of this book.

The primary purpose of this Bible study is to help you to take a fresh look at retirement, reevaluate your current situation, and consider making some changes.

This book contains six Bible study sessions on the topic of retirement that can be done individually or in a small group. The studies are written for people who have never studied the Bible, occasionally study the Bible, or often study the Bible. That is, virtually everyone interested in retirement will benefit from these studies. Each session allows the Bible to speak to where you are and where God may want you to go.

While these studies can be done individually, they are primarily designed to be done in a small group setting. In fact, you will receive maximum benefit when the study is discussed in a group. The more diverse your group is in age and experience, the more you will learn from these studies.

SUGGESTIONS ON FORMING A GROUP

1. Form a group that has between eight and 15 members. Groups larger or smaller are generally less effective.

2. One person should be appointed as the group facilitator. The facilitator's primary role is to get everyone together at an appointed time and place. The facilitator also gets the study started and keeps it going without getting off track. After the initial meeting the facilitator role can rotate within the group.

3. At the first meeting have the group members introduce themselves to one another and have each person share his or her responses to the following questions:

a) Where were you born and raised?

a) Where were you born and raised?

b) Where were you and what were you doing at age 10? Age 18? Age 25?

c) What one person, place, or experience has had the greatest impact on your life and why?

4. Before starting the study group members should agree on the length and frequency of meeting times. Normally, each study should take about one hour. All group members should commit themselves to attending all group sessions, unless there are circumstances beyond their control.

5. Give time for the small group to gel. Don't expect everything to click in the first session or two.

Because the interaction in a small group can reach into personal areas, it is important that group members agree upon "ground rules."

SUGGESTED GROUND RULES FOR SMALL GROUP STUDY

1. Jesus said that "the Holy Spirit, whom the Father will send in my name, will teach you all things and will remind you of everything I said to you." With this in mind, each group session should open in prayer asking the Holy Spirit to teach and guide. (Not everyone needs to pray. If a person is uncomfortable praying in public, he or she should be given freedom to remain silent.)

2. No one or two persons should dominate the discussion time. All group members should have an equal opportunity to express their thoughts, feelings, and experiences.

3. Because people's experiences and perspectives vary, there will be ideas, thoughts, and feelings expressed which will be quite diverse. All members should respect one another's perspective.

4. Confidentiality on what is said in the study should be agreed upon by all group members.

5. If significant conflict arises between specific group members, they should make every effort to resolve this conflict apart from group time. That is, they should agree to meet together at another time to discuss their differences.

6. If the group ends in prayer, members should pray for one another.

SESSION 1 | WHAT IS RETIREMENT?

INTRODUCTION
Have one or more group members read the introduction aloud.

The Issue: As followers of Jesus Christ, do we really understand retirement?

When defining most terms and concepts, the dictionary is a logical place to begin. Dictionaries define retirement as:

1. the leaving of job or career: the act of leaving a job or career at or near the usual age for doing so, or the state of having left a job or career

2. the time after having stopped working: the time that follows the end of somebody's working life

3. being away from busy life: a state of being withdrawn from the rest of the world or from a former busy life

Retirement, as we know it today, is a relatively new idea. For centuries people worked hard to survive and rarely lived long enough to consider retirement. In fact, those who lived into old age did not retire, but found less strenuous ways to contribute to the survival of their household. The extended family usually took care of the needs of members who could no longer work.

As Americans began to move from farms to cities during the Industrial Revolution, lifelong work no longer became possible. Since most of the work in factories was physical, companies let older workers go and replaced them with younger, more able-bodied employees. The combination of "forced retirement" and the Great Depression led Franklin D. Roosevelt to sign the Social Security Act of 1935. Since most workers did not live to the eligibility age of 65, this legislation was not as progressive as it seems to us now.

After World War II American businesses started to boom and life expectancy continued to grow. In addition to Social Security, many large companies began to offer private pensions for their employees and modern retirement began to emerge on the American landscape. The first generation, and perhaps only generation, to benefit from the convergence of Social Security, pensions, private retirement accounts, and other sources of retirement income is the Silent Generation. (This generation was born between 1925 and 1943, give or take a few years.) The Silent Generation had the good fortune of working at a time when they could stay with the same company for 30, 35, or more years and retire with a significant retirement cushion. No generation before them, and probably no generation after, will be able to retire like the Silents. Though the Silents' retirement course is an anomaly, the investment/retirement industry has marketed it as the norm.

Recent surveys have indicated that the Boomer Generation (which follows the Silents) will not retire to Sun City or The Villages in the numbers the Silent Generation members have. Many Boomers plan to and will need to stay in the game. While many new retirees will leave their jobs and careers, they will find other meaningful activities to give their lives purpose. In retirement Boomers will play golf and take cruises, but they will also start new businesses and nonprofit organizations, volunteer by using their experience and expertise, and find other ways of "giving back."

So, retirement now and in the near future will be less a time to withdraw for "rest and relaxation" and more a time to engage and stay in the game to be "retired and rewired."

YOUR TAKE

From the following list, check the responses that best describes your definition of retirement. Discuss your responses with your group.

__ Retirement is a time to slow down and withdraw from the rat race.
__ Retirement is a reward for years of hard work.

__ Retirement is a time when you are put on a shelf.
__ Retirement is a time to reflect on the meaning of life.
__ Retirement is a time brought on by health problems and aging.
__ Retirement is a time when a person can give back.
__ Retirement is a time when you can finally spend quality time
with your family.
__ Retirement is a time to play.
__ Retirement is a time to start a new adventure.
__ Retirement is an unfortunate time forced on you by other
people.
__ Retirement is a time to finish off your bucket list.
__ Retirement is a time to see the world.
__ Retirement is a very boring time.
__ Retirement is a time to use your experience, talents, skills, and
wisdom in helping others.
__ Other _____.

Why did you answer the way you did?

YOUR REFLECTION
Read the following passages from the Bible and answer the
questions that follow.

Unless the LORD builds the house, the builders labor in vain.
Unless the LORD watches over the city, the guards stand watch in vain.
In vain you rise early and stay up late, toiling for food to eat—for he
grants sleep to those he loves.
—Psalm 127: 1, 2

1. What do these verses say about work?

2. What role does our relationship with God play in our work?

There remains, then, a Sabbath-rest for the people of God; for anyone who enters God's rest also rests from their works, just as God did from his. Let us, therefore, make every effort to enter that rest, so that no one will perish by following their example of disobedience.
—Hebrews 4:9-11

3. What do these verses say about rest?

4. What role does our relationship with God play in our rest?

Remember the Sabbath day by keeping it holy. Six days you shall labor and do all your work, but the seventh day is a sabbath to the Lord your God. On it you shall not do any work, neither you, nor your son or daughter, nor your male or female servant, nor your animals, nor any foreigner residing in your towns. For in six days the Lord made the heavens and the earth, the sea, and all that is in them, but he rested on the seventh day. Therefore the Lord blessed the Sabbath day and made it holy.
—Exodus 20:8-11

5. In what ways is the Sabbath day similar to retirement? In what ways is it different?

6. Do you believe that retirement should be a cessation of work? If so, why? If not, why not?

YOUR APPLICATION

During this coming week do the following exercises to help you better understand your attitudes and understanding of retirement.

1. Think about and write down your attitudes toward retirement. From what sources did you get your attitudes and understanding of retirement?

2. Talk to someone, preferably a friend, who is retired. Ask them some of the following questions:

a) Were you adequately prepared for retirement?

b) Was retirement hard or easy for you? Why?

c) Were there any surprises in retirement that caught you off guard?

d) Is there anything about your retirement that you would do differently?

SESSION 2 | RETIREMENT AND THE BIBLE

INTRODUCTION
Have one or more group members read the introduction aloud.

The Issue: What does the Bible say about retirement?

Retirement is an important topic, so we might naturally go to the Bible to see what it says about the subject. Interestingly enough, the Bible says almost nothing about retirement. The closest reference is found in the eighth chapter of the book of Numbers. There we read:

The LORD said to Moses, "This applies to the Levites: Men twenty-five years old or more shall come to take part in the work at the Tent of Meeting, but at the age of fifty, they must retire from their regular service and work no longer. They may assist their brothers in performing their duties at the Tent of Meeting, but they themselves must not do the work. This, then, is how you are to assign the responsibilities of the Levites."
—Numbers 8: 23-26

While this passage refers directly to the Levites, (members of the Israelite tribe that performed priestly and religious duties) it reveals that God considers retirement as valid. Yet, the passage seems to be descriptive of the Levites' situation and not a broad endorsement of retirement for all. In fact, Abraham, Moses, Samuel, Simeon, Anna and other biblical characters did not retire, but continued in their calling until old age and death.

Still scripture makes it clear that periods of rest are important. There are numerous examples and exhortations concerning rest. After creating the universe, God rested on the seventh day; we are to remember the Sabbath and keep it holy through rest; Jesus often withdrew from pressing crowds to rest and pray; we are instructed to rest and to come to Jesus for rest; and even the land was to rest from continuous planting. But the Bible does not equate rest with retirement.

It must be noted that the lifestyle in biblical times differed considerably from our own. People worked hard to maintain survival and leisure needed to be grabbed in bits and pieces. Leisure and a leisurely retirement is a recent phenomenon. In biblical times only the rich and powerful (with slaves) could regularly experience leisure. In addition, it is quite clear that when Jesus said "follow me", it was for a lifetime. Certainly followers of Jesus Christ are not called to a mindless retirement of leisure activities. We are called to stay engaged in loving and serving God and the people he has created. This engagement in our faith in Jesus Christ is an active, not passive, endeavor.

YOUR TAKE

From the following list check the statements that you believe best expresses God's and the Bible's view of retirement. Discuss your response(s) with your group.

___ I think God doesn't care how we spend our retirement years.

___ I think we spend too much time wondering what God thinks; we have no clue.

___ I think God "customizes" retirement for each of us.

___ I think God wants us to enjoy our retirement, since we have worked so hard.

___ I think God wants us to pray and find the ways He wants us to spend our retirement years.

___ I think God wants us to continue loving and serving Him and others in retirement.

___ I don't think the Bible or God has any relevance to retirement.

YOUR REFLECTION

Read the following passages from the Bible and answer the questions that follow.

The LORD said to Moses, "This applies to the Levites: Men twenty-five years old or more shall come to take part in the work at the Tent of Meeting, but at the age of fifty, they must retire from their regular service and work no longer. They may assist their brothers in performing their duties at the Tent of Meeting, but they themselves must not do the work. This, then, is how you are to assign the responsibilities of the Levites."
—Numbers 8: 23-26

1. Do you think this passage is descriptive (describes the Levites situation only) or prescriptive (instructions on retirement for all of us)? Why did you answer as you did?

2. Why do you think the Levites were given a specific age, in this case the age of 50, to stop working?

3. What might be the difference between doing the work and just assisting? How might these instructions relate to our retirement years?

Even when I am old and gray, do not forsake me, my God, till I declare your power to the next generation, your mighty acts to all who are to come.
—Psalm 71:18

4. In old age and retirement, what "job" does God give us?

5. What opportunities do you have to speak into the lives of the younger generations? How do you successfully communicate the gospel to younger people?

YOUR APPLICATION

During the coming week spend at least 15 minutes a day praying (talking to God) about how you should spend your retirement years. To help you, here are some questions to guide your prayer time.

1. Lord, how do you want me to use my retirement years?

2. Lord, what gifts, abilities, talents, experiences, and wisdom have you given me that I can put to use in retirement?

3. Lord, what is the next step you want me to take now?

SESSION 3 | RETIREMENT REVISITED

INTRODUCTION
Have one or more group members read the introduction aloud.

The Issue: Is it time for us to take a fresh look at retirement?

Attitudes toward retirement are changing...and changing rather quickly. Numerous factors have led to this attitudinal shift, especially among the Boomer Generation. Now, people are living longer, staying healthy longer, and, if retiring at age 65, may experience 25 years or more of retirement. What will you do for 25 years? Will your money hold out? To complicate matters, Social Security funds appear to be drying up.

In addition, Boomers are not aging without some kicking and screaming. They want to stay in the game as long as possible and still have an impact and influence in our society. According to The New Retirement Survey commissioned by Merrill Lynch, most Boomers are not interested in pursuing a traditional retirement of leisure. Some highlights of the survey found that:

- 76% of Boomers plan to continue to work and earn even after they "retire" from their current job or career.

- Since the retirement baseline age of 65 was established, life expectancy has increased by over seven years.

- Most Boomers reject a life of either full-time leisure or full-time work.

- For Boomers it's not about the money. While continued earnings are important, most Boomers want to keep working for the mental stimulation and challenge.

- The Boomers are being transformed from a "me" generation into a "we" generation. That is, they now have deep concerns for the well-being of their children, grandchildren, parents, and their community.

- The unpredictable cost of illness and healthcare is by far Boomers greatest fear.

- Boomer women are dreaming of retiring to Mars while Boomer men hope to retire to Venus. That is, Boomer men are looking to work less, relax more, and spend more time with their spouse. By contrast, Boomer women see empty nesting and retirement as new opportunities for career development, community involvement, and continued personal growth.

- Financial preparedness is the gateway to retirement freedom and the antidote to retirement phobia.

YOUR TAKE

Read and answer each of the following questions. Discuss your responses with your group.

1. Which one of the following statements best explains why you retired or want to retire?

___ I've worked long enough and now it's time to play.
___ I reached/will reach the mandatory retirement age.
___ My job was/will be eliminated.
___ I was/will be replaced by a younger person.
___ I retired for health reasons.
___ My company moved and I didn't want to follow.
___ I have reached all my career goals.
___ I took/will take advantage of an early retirement option.
___ My work was/is boring; I wanted/want to move on to new
    things.
___ Other _____.

2. Which one of the following statements best describes your attitude toward retirement?

___ I finally have/will have the time to do things I've put off.

___ I feel/will feel like I've been "put out to pasture."

___ I have/will have too much time on my hands.

___ I have/will have no trouble filling my day with worthwhile and enjoyable activities.

___ I love/will love the freedom it has given/will give me.

___ I feel it is/will be my reward for many years of hard work and sacrifice.

___ I find/will find it to be a financial struggle.

___ I feel retirement has exceeded/will exceed my expectations.

___ Other _____.

YOUR REFLECTION

Read Ecclesiastes 2:17-26 and answer the questions that follow:

So I hated life, because the work that is done under the sun was grievous to me. All of it is meaningless, a chasing after the wind. I hated all the things I had toiled for under the sun, because I must leave them to the one who comes after me. And who knows whether he will be a wise man or a fool? Yet he will have control over all the work into which I have poured my effort and skill under the sun. This too is meaningless. So my heart began to despair over all my toilsome labor under the sun. For a man may do his work with wisdom, knowledge and skill, and then he must leave all he owns to someone who has not worked for it. This too is meaningless and a great misfortune. What does a man get for all the toil and anxious striving with which he labors under the sun? All his days his work is pain and grief; even at night his mind does not rest. This too is meaningless. A man can do nothing better than to eat and drink and find satisfaction in his work. This too, I see, is from the hand of God, for without him, who can eat or find enjoyment? To the

man who pleases him, God gives wisdom, knowledge and happiness, but to the sinner he gives the task of gathering and storing up wealth to hand it over to the one who pleases God. This too is meaningless, a chasing after the wind.
—Ecclesiastes 2:17-26

Background: The author of Ecclesiastes, called the teacher, is probably King Solomon. He addresses the futility of life based on self-centered choices. Despite enormous achievement, the writer wrestles to find meaning in his work but finds little.

Too many people come to retirement questioning the value of their years of labor. Often a retiree will numb the meaninglessness of life with pleasure. And like the writer of Ecclesiastes, some retirees may find both work and pleasure to be empty without God.

1. How would you describe the attitude of the teacher in this passage?

___ He is depressed.

___ He is angry.

___ He is frustrated.

___ He is in despair.

___ He is angry with God.

___ He is angry with himself for being so stupid.

___ He is confused.

___ He is numb.

___ He is disillusioned.

___ He is cynical.

2. Do you identify with any of these feelings? If so, which one(s) and why?

3. If you were to compare your attitude toward work to the teacher's attitude, how would it compare?

__ I found my years of work to be quite meaningful and enjoyable.

__ My attitudes towards work are similar to the teacher's.

__ I found much more meaning in my work than he did.

__ My work wasn't/isn't that important to me.

__ I didn't/don't find the meaning of my life in my work.

__ Like the teacher, I found work to be toil and quite meaningless.

__ Other _____.

4. How do you feel about leaving "the fruits of your labor" to somebody else?

5. Do you agree with the statement that "a man (or woman) can do nothing better than to eat and drink and find satisfaction in his/her work?" Please explain your response.

6. What makes your life meaningful?

YOUR APPLICATION

Answer the following questions and this week begin to apply your responses.

1. In what ways is your relationship with God in retirement different than it was before retirement? Or, in what ways do you think your relationship with God in retirement will be different then it is now?

2. We know that followers of Jesus never retire. What do you think God wants you to do with your remaining years?

3. What changes do you need to make in your life to do what you think God wants you to do?

SESSION 4 | RETIREMENT INVESTMENTS

INTRODUCTION

Have one or more group members read the introduction aloud.

The Issue: How good are your retirement investments?

If retirement is about anything, it is about investments. Most retirees have invested much. They've invested their money in preparation for retirement. They've invested energy, resources, and time in their work with the hope that they will have some time to "play." If married, they have invested much in their marriages. And if a parent, retirees continue to invest in their children and perhaps, grandchildren. Retirees understand what the term delayed gratification means and what it means to wait for a return on investment.

For many retirees these investments in their future bring some anxiety. Will I have enough money to live comfortably? Will I outlive my retirement resources? Will I stagnate as a person? Will my retirement life be satisfying enough? Will my family life bring joy or sorrow? And many other anxious questions and concerns.

Retirement is a major time of transition that can either be a time of great satisfaction and fulfillment or a time of decline, frustration, and discouragement. How you negotiate your retirement years often depends on the kind of investments you make. Certainly, financial investments are important in retirement, but they are not the only important investments. Making investments in your health is important. Making investments in your relationships is important. Making investments in your spiritual life is important. Making investments in serving Christ and others is important.

In this session we will study one of Jesus' parables which addresses investing and investments. Initially, this parable seems to be about investing money. But Jesus is addressing more than financial investments. He is teaching us about how we should invest our lives. So, let's move into the study and see what we can learn from the ultimate investment counselor.

YOUR TAKE

Read and answer each of the following questions. Discuss your response with your group.

1. If you had to do it over again, how would you prepare differently for retirement?

___ I wouldn't do anything differently.

___ I would've paced myself better.

___ I would've invested more time in physical fitness.

___ I would've spent more time with my family.

___ I would've saved and invested more money.

___ I would've taken more risks.

___ I would've invested more time and energy in my spiritual life.

___ I would've invested more time in my marriage and/or friendships.

___ I would've developed more hobbies or a "serious avocation."

___ I would've gotten more education.

___ I would've worked less and played more.

___ Other _____.

YOUR REFLECTION

Read Matthew 25:14-30 and answer the questions that follow.

Again, it will be like a man going on a journey, who called his servants and entrusted his property to them. To one he gave five talents of money, to another two talents, and to another one talent, each according to his ability. Then he went on his journey.

The man who had received the five talents went at once and put his money to work and gained five more. So also, the one with the two talents gained two more. But the man who had received the one talent went off, dug a hole in the ground and hid his master's money.

After a long time the master of those servants returned and settled accounts with them. The man who had received the five talents brought the other five. 'Master,' he said, 'you entrusted me with five talents. See, I have gained five more.' "His master replied, 'Well done, good and faithful servant! You have been faithful with a few things; I will put you in charge of many things. Come and share your master's happiness!'

The man with the two talents also came 'Master,' he said, 'you entrusted me with two talents; see, I have gained two more.' "His master replied, 'Well done, good and faithful servant! You have been faithful with a few things; I will put you in charge of many things. Come and share your master's happiness!'

Then the man who had received the one talent came. 'Master,' he said, 'I knew that you are a hard man, harvesting where you have not sown and gathering where you have not scattered seed. So I was afraid and went out and hid your talent in the ground. See, here is what belongs to you.'

His master replied, 'You wicked, lazy servant! So you knew that I harvest where I have not sown and gather where I have not scattered seed? Well then, you should have put my money on deposit with the bankers, so that when I returned I would have received it back with interest. Take the talent from him and give it to the one who has the ten talents.

For everyone who has will be given more, and he will have an abundance. Whoever does not have, even what he has will be taken from him. And throw that worthless servant outside, into the darkness, where there will be weeping and gnashing of teeth.'
—Matthew 25:14-30

Background: Jesus' characteristic method of teaching was through parables. Some entire chapters in the Gospels are devoted to Jesus' parables, as we have here in Matthew 25. Although parables are often memorable stories that impress the listener with a clear picture of the truth, even the disciples were sometimes confused as to the meaning of the parables. Most of Jesus' parables have one central point. In finding the central point of the parable, the Bible student needs to discover the meaning the parable had in the time of Jesus. We need to relate the parable to Jesus' proclamation of the kingdom of God and to his miracles. In general, Jesus' parables are a call to a radical decision to follow him, regardless of the cost. (from Nelson's Illustrated Bible Dictionary)

Note: In Jesus' day, a talent was a measurement of weight for silver and gold. It is estimated that one talent (3000 shekels) was about 34 kg or 75 pounds.

1. In this parable, what is the master's attitude towards investing and investments?

2. Why do you think the master entrusted his money to the servants? Why do you think the master did not give the same amount of money to each of the three servants?

3. Why do you think the master praised and rewarded the first two servants the same, even though one had more responsibility than the other?

4. Why do you think the third servant behaved differently than the other two?

5. What part do you think risk played in this parable? Do you think the master liked risk-taking? Please explain your response.

6. In this parable, who is the master? Who are the servants? With which one of the servants do you identify? Why?

7. Which of the following statements best summarizes the parable?

___ If you don't invest wisely, you'll lose out.

___ If you don't look after the master's affairs, you will be punished.

___ God has given all of us talents and he wants us to invest them wisely.

___ Taking risks for Jesus is not really taking risks at all.

___ All of us will ultimately be judged on how we invest our lives.

___ Making money is the most important thing we can do.

___ No investment/ no return is as true in the Christian life as any-where else.

___ We should not be afraid to serve Jesus; instead we should serve him enthusiastically.

YOUR APPLICATION

During the coming week, reflect and act on the following questions.

1. In what ways are you afraid to take a risk for Jesus Christ?

2. In what ways do you think Jesus wants you to invest your talents?

3. What practical steps do you need to take and what changes do you need to make in your life in order to see a greater ROI (return on investment) for God's kingdom?

SESSION 5 | CAN AND ABLE

INTRODUCTION
Have one or more group members read the introduction aloud.

The Issue: Are we still of any use in retirement?

Retirement can be a time of reflection as we look back over our lives. Upon reflection we may find our lives to be quite satisfying: a successful career; a family raised; many good friendships; good financial security; many years of service to others. But reflecting on our lives may also bring disappointment and regret—never reaching your career goals; children who did not turn out as you wished; some broken relationships; not having enough money; a lingering lack of purpose and meaning in life.

Yet, there can be more. Our retirement years do not need to be a time when we put our talents, gifts, abilities, and experiences on the shelf. Instead, we should explore unique ways to integrate retirement's leisurely slowdown with productive activities. Especially for Christians, retirement should not be a time of allowing our God-given resources to atrophy and whither. In fact, it is often in retirement years that many Christians become more productive and effective for God's kingdom. Retirees possess a wealth of experience and wisdom that is greatly needed in today's chaotic world. As a retiree, God wants you to use your unique gifts, abilities, and experiences to minister to others.

Throughout the Bible we see examples of various people using their abilities and experience in unique ways to serve God. Noah was a shipbuilder. Esau was a hunter. Naomi was a judge. King David was a poet. Luke was a physician. Several of Jesus' disciples were professional fishermen, abilities that were quite valuable as they traveled and ministered. The apostle Paul was a tent maker. Jesus was a carpenter.

As we get to know and understand the abilities and talents that God has given us, we are better able to use them in service to his kingdom. The development and use of our abilities in serving God are directly related to our growth as Christians. And retirement is not a time to stop growing in our relationship with God. The Bible is full of examples of people who allowed their abilities and talents to be stretched by God. Moses served God in many powerful ways as he took risks to develop his ability as a leader. David progressed from a shepherd boy to musician to fighter to king. Nehemiah grew from the cupbearer of the king to the rebuilder of Jerusalem's walls. Peter moved from fisherman to Jesus' inner circle of disciples to a leader of the early church.

In this session you will have an opportunity to rediscover the unique talents, abilities, gifts, and experiences God has given to you. You will also have the opportunity to begin exploring new ways God may want you to use these resources.

YOUR TAKE
Read and answer the following questions:

1. Do you believe there is prejudice against older people in our society? Please explain your response.

2. Which one of the following statements do you think best describes what most younger people think about older people?

___ Older adults use too many of society's resources and give little back.

___ Older people should be shown respect.

___ Older people should only drive between 9am and 3pm.

___ Older people are ruining our economy through Social Security and Medicare.

___ I wish older people would help me figure out life.

__ We are wasting the talent, experience, and wisdom of older people because they are isolated from younger people.

__ Older people have needs and concerns like the rest of us.

__ Other _____.

3. Which one of the following statements do you think best describes what most older people think about younger people?

__ Younger people are clueless.

__ Younger people have a lot to learn, but don't listen.

__ Younger people are no different than we were at their age.

__ Younger people have a much harder time figuring out life than we did at their age.

__ Younger people are lazy and would rather play than work.

__ I don't understand younger people.

__ I think younger people are wonderful.

__ Younger people can use the wisdom of us older folks.

__ Other _____.

YOUR REFLECTION

Read the following passages and answer the questions that follow.

There are different kinds of gifts, but the same Spirit. There are different kinds of service, but the same Lord. There are different kinds of working, but the same God works all of them in all men.
Now to each one the manifestation of the Spirit is given for the common good. To one there is given through the Spirit the message of wisdom, to another the message of knowledge by means of the same Spirit, to another faith by the same Spirit, to another gifts of healing by that one Spirit, to another miraculous powers, to another prophecy, to another distinguishing between spirits, to another speaking in different kinds of tongues, and to still another the interpretation of tongues.

All these are the work of one and the same Spirit, and he gives them to each one, just as he determines. The body is a unit, though it is made up of many parts; and though all its parts are many, they form one body. So it is with Christ.
—*Corinthians 12:4-12*

1. According to these verses, what is the source of our gifts, talents, and abilities?

2. Which of the following statements best describes why Christians have been given spiritual gifts?

___ So we can know who is the most spiritually mature among us

___ So that the church, the body of Christ, can be more effective in ministry

___ So that we can have differing theological views on spiritual gifts

___ So that Christians can experience unity in the presence of diversity

___ So that the power of the Holy Spirit can be seen in tangible ways

___ So that God can show his love to us, his children

___ So that the body of Christ, the church, may be more spiritually whole

3. Realizing that these verses do not give us an exhaustive list of spiritual gifts, what is your spiritual gift or gifts? How do you use this gift/these gifts in your life?

4. Which of the following statements best describes the relationship between your life's motivation and your spiritual life?

__ I am not motivated by spiritual concerns.

__ I am motivated to become as spiritually mature as possible.

__ I am motivated to have an intimate relationship with Jesus Christ.

__ I am motivated to live my life as Christ-like as possible.

__ I am motivated to get to heaven and avoid hell.

__ I am motivated to be a good person and make the world a better place.

5. Which of the following statements best summarizes these verses?

__ We need to work together to build up the body of Christ.

__ We have been given individual gifts, talents, and abilities to help further God's kingdom on earth.

__ Unity within the church, the body of Christ, should be achieved at all cost.

__ While God gives us special gifts and abilities, his Spirit is in control of his church.

__ With Christ as the head, the church has been given spiritual gifts and power to minister to a broken world.

__ Spiritual gifts have been given to us for the good of the whole church.

YOUR APPLICATION

During the coming week, reflect and act on the following questions.

1. What gifts, talents, abilities, and experiences do you have that you can put to use to further God's kingdom? What do you do well? Write down your responses. Think, and pray about them.

2. In what practical ways can you put your God-given resources to work to minister to others. List some areas of possible ministry activity or service that might fit who you are.

SESSION **6** | FINISHING WELL

INTRODUCTION
Have one or more group members read the introduction aloud.

The Issue: How do we finish life well in the time we have left?

For many, retirement means slowing down, kicking back, and doing what you want when you want to do it. Certainly many retirees feel they have earned this right. But retirees who are followers of Jesus must ask themselves: How does God want me to live my remaining years here on earth? How should I spend my time and energy to serve God as he wants me to? How can I finish well?

The apostle Paul knew what it meant to finish well. In 2 Timothy 4:7 and 8 he wrote, "I fought the good fight, I finished the race, I have kept the faith. Now there is in store for me the crown of righteousness, which the Lord, the righteous Judge, will reward to me on that day—and not only to me, but also to all who have longed for his appearing." Several times in his writings Paul used the metaphor of life as a race. In Acts 20:23, 24 he wrote as he faced possible persecution and abuse, "I only know that in every city the Holy Spirit warns me that prison and hardships are facing me. However, I consider my life worth nothing to me, if only I may finish the race and complete the task the Lord Jesus has given me—the task of testifying to the gospel of God's grace."

In Hebrews 12:1 and 2 the apostle Paul made it clear why we are to run this race for Jesus Christ. "Therefore, since we are surrounded by such a great cloud of witnesses, let us throw off everything that hinders and the sin that so easily entangles, and let us run with perseverance the race marked out for us. Let us fix our eyes on Jesus, the author and perfecter of our faith, who for the joy set before him endured the cross, scorning its shame, and sat down at the right hand of the throne of God."

Retirement is a time when we should reassess why and how we are running the race of life. For Christians it is clear that we are to finish well in the race of life. We are called to focus on a life devoted to

Jesus Christ. We are instructed to live out our love for Christ through tangible acts of Christ-like behavior. Jesus told us what it means to finish well when he instructed us to "worship the Lord our God, and serve him only."

Serving God can take many forms. For example, we are instructed in Romans 12 to "be devoted to one another in brotherly love. Honor one another above ourselves. Never be lacking in zeal, but keep your spiritual fervor, serving the Lord. Be joyful in hope, patient in affliction, faithful in prayer. Share with God's people who are in need. Practice hospitality." In reality, most of us know more about serving God and others than we could live out in a lifetime.

In this session we will look at two passages from the Bible that address the race of life and serving God. This session will also help you think through specific ways you can use your gifts, abilities, and experiences in concrete service to God. Allow yourself to be open and creative as you bring fresh thoughts, ideas, and feelings to your retirement experience.

YOUR TAKE

Read and answer each of the following questions. Discuss your responses with your group.

1. A legacy is something handed down from one generation to another. Which one of the following statements best describes the legacy you want to leave?

___ I would like to be known as a kind and wise person.

___ I would like to leave a legacy which helps the poor.

___ I would like to be known as a very good business person.

___ I would like to leave a legacy of Christian wisdom and growth to my children and grandchildren.

___ I would like to be known as a spiritually mature person.

__ I would like to leave a legacy of making the world a better place than I found it.

__ I would like to be known as a person who took risks for Jesus Christ.

__ I would like to be known as a person who invested myself in others.

__ I would like to be known as a person who really knew what it meant to follow Jesus Christ.

__ Other _____.

YOUR REFLECTION

Read following passages and answer the questions that follow.

Do you not know that in a race all the runners run, but only one gets the prize? Run in such a way as to get the prize. Everyone who competes in the games goes into strict training. They do it to get a crown that will not last; but we do it to get a crown that will last forever.

Therefore I do not run like a man running aimlessly; I do not fight like a man beating the air. No, I beat my body and make it my slave so that after I have preached to others, I myself will not be disqualified for the prize.
—1 Corinthians 9:24-27

1. Do you see your life as a race to run and finish well? If so, why? If not, why not?

2. What is the prize which Paul writes about here?

3. For Christians, what is the primary purpose(s) of the race of life?

Then the mother of Zebedee's sons came to Jesus with her sons and, kneeling down, asked a favor of him. "What is it you want?" he asked. She said, "Grant that one of these two sons of mine may sit at your right and the other at your left in your kingdom." "You don't know what you are asking," Jesus said to them. "Can you drink the cup I am going to drink?" "We can," they answered. Jesus said to them, "You will indeed drink from my cup, but to sit at my right or left is not for me to grant. These places belong to those for whom they have been prepared by my Father."

When the ten heard about this, they were indignant with the two brothers. Jesus called them together and said, 'You know that the rulers of the Gentiles lord it over them, and their high officials exercise authority over them. Not so with you. Instead, whoever wants to become great among you must be your servant, and whoever wants to be first must be your slave--just as the Son of Man did not come to be served, but to serve, and to give his life as a ransom for many.'
—Matthew 20:20-28

4. How do you think Jesus Christ felt about the mother's request?

__ He anticipated her request and was ready to respond.

__ He was annoyed with her aggressiveness.

__ He understood the hearts of human beings, so nothing surprised him.

__ He was patient and understanding.

__ He realized it was another opportunity to teach.

__ He was angry and disgusted.

5. Why do you think the other disciples were angry with the two brothers?

6. What was Jesus' definition of greatness?

7. In what practical ways are we to apply Jesus' example of service and servanthood?

YOUR APPLICATION

During this coming week reflect and act on these following exercises.

1. List those gifts, abilities, skills, talent, expertise, knowledge, experiences, influences, etc. that you can bring to serving God and his kingdom. (This may seem like repetition, but we have given you time to think more deeply about how God has made you and for what reasons.)

2. In which of the following areas can these qualities and capabilities be put to practical service?

__ Helping to provide mercy ministries, i.e. food, clothing, housing, etc.

__ Sharing the gospel with others

__ Ministering to the homeless

__ Using your computer/IT skills to minister

__ Helping tutor or mentor young people

__ Providing help to start businesses as ministries

__ Teaching the Bible and/or other subject matter to others

__ Helping with mission activities around the world

__ Providing leadership in your church or other ministry organizations

__ Assisting ministries in managing their resources better

__ Helping ministries to plan strategically

__ Providing hands-on help, such as rehab/remodeling work

__ Helping in fundraising

__ Other _____.

3. Which is the following ministry opportunities might be of interest to you?

__ food/clothing bank	__ grief ministry
__ housing ministry	__ athletic ministry
__ tutoring inner city children	__ camping ministry
__ international student ministry	__ campus ministry
__ children ministry	__ family ministry
__ marriage ministry	__ teaching ministry
__ urban ministry	__ music ministry
__ media ministry	__ computer ministry
__ counseling ministry	__ men's/women's ministry
__ parenting ministry	__ mentoring ministry
__ unwed mothers ministry	__ substance-abuse ministry

__ prison ministry   __ prayer ministry

__ employment ministry   __ singles ministry

__ evangelism ministry   __ marketplace ministry

__ adoption/foster care ministry   __ human trafficking ministry

__ art ministry   __ seniors ministry

__ nursing home ministry   __ MothersOfPre-Schoolers

__ creating a new ministry to_____

4. Now based upon your responses in the above check lists, determine who or what organization you need to contact to take the next step in your race to finish well for Jesus Christ. If you do not know where to go for a next step, talk to your pastor or the church staff person who oversees your outreach ministries. You can also do a search online to find the organizations in your area that are doing the type of ministry you desire.

Remember! No follower of Jesus Christ is retired, but we are all called to be rewired!

FURTHER READING

Retire Retirement: Career Strategies for the Boomer Generation by Tamara Erickson

Rethinking Retirement: Finishing Life for the Glory of Christ by John Piper

Living with Purpose in a Worn-Out Body: Spiritual Encouragement for Older Adults by Missy Buchanan

Don't Retire, Rewire! By Jeri Sedlar and Rick Miners

The Second-Half Adventure: Don't Just Retire--Use Your Time, Resources & Skills to Change the World by Kay Marshall Strom

101 Ways to Reinvest Your Life by Steve Sjogren, Janie Sjogren

ABOUT THE AUTHOR

Peter Menconi has written and presented widely on generational and aging issues. His rich background as a dentist, pastor, counselor, business owner, conference speaker, husband, father, and grandfather brings unique perspectives to his writing.

Born and raised in Chicago, Pete graduated from the University of Illinois, College of Dentistry and practiced dentistry for 23 years in private practice, in the U.S. Army and in a mission hospital in Kenya, East Africa. In addition, Pete has a M.S. in Counseling Psychology and several years of seminary training. He has also been a commodity futures floor trader, a speaker with the American Dental Association, and a broker of medical and dental practices.

For over 20 years Pete was the outreach pastor at a large church in suburban Denver, Colorado. Currently, he is the president of Mt. Sage Publishing and board member with the CASA Network.

Pete's writings include the book *The Intergenerational Church: Understanding Congregations from WWII to www.com*, The Support Group Series, a 9-book Bible study series, and numerous articles.

Pete and his wife Jean live in the Denver area and they are the parents of 3 adult children and the grandparents of 9 grandchildren.

Pete Menconi can be reached at petermenconi@msn.com.

CASA NETWORK

AGING WELL

BIBLESTUDYSERIES

Finally, a Bible study series for everyone 50 and over
who wants to stay in the game as long as possible!

THE AGING CHALLENGE

The primary purpose of this Bible study is to
help you take a fresh look at aging, reevaluate
your current situation, and consider making
some changes.

THE NEW R & R: RETIRED AND REWIRED

The primary purpose of this Bible study is to
help you to take a fresh look at retirement,
reevaluate your current situation, and consider
making some changes.

GENERATIONS TOGETHER

The primary purpose of this Bible study is to
help you to take a fresh look at our current
generations, how the generations relate, and
how we can be better together.

Available at www.Amazon.com

SAGE OR CURMUDGEON

The primary purpose of this Bible study is to help you to take a closer look at your attitude about aging, how to reevaluate your attitude, and how to move toward becoming a sage for younger people.

THE AGING FAMILY AND MARRIAGE

The primary purpose of this Bible study is to help you to take a closer look at your aging marriage and/or family and see how you can maximize these relationships.

FINISHING WELL

The primary purpose of this Bible study is to help you to take a closer look at how you can finish well before your life is over.

Available at www.Amazon.com

THE INTERGENERATIONAL CHURCH:
Understanding Congregations from
WWII to www.com

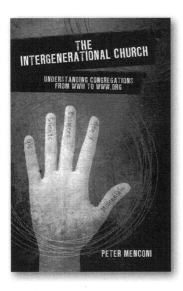

Are certain generations underrepresented in your church?

Would you like to see more young adults in your congregation?

The Intergenerational Church: Understanding Congregations from WWII to www.com will show you why understanding today's generations is crucial for the survival and thrival of the local church.

The Intergenerational Church is a breakthrough book that will help you meet the Intergenerational Challenge.

FROM THIS IMPORTANT BOOK, YOU WILL LEARN HOW TO:

- Minimize generational tension.
- Get all the generations moving in the same direction.
- Develop leaders from all generations.
- Deliver intergenerational preaching.
- Cultivate intergenerational worship and community.
- Stimulate intergenerational mission and outreach.

Available at www.Amazon.com

8349589R00035

Made in the USA
San Bernardino, CA
06 February 2014